Reviewers and pastoral leaders of many denominations have applauded the contributions made by Debra Hintz in her first book, *Prayer Services for Parish Meetings* (Twenty-Third Publications).

"...will be a big help, especially for those who hold the ideal of building a service around the Scriptures but cannot always manage the time to locate and select desirable passages."

Sharon M. Guevin
Church Teachers

"...helps being small or large group sessions in a prayerful manner appropriate to the season of the year."

Nat'l Federation of
Christian Life Communities

"...appropriate for setting the tone and prayerful environment for various meetings and gatherings."

Aids in Ministry

"Prayer services weren't even mentioned in my seminary days, so this practical volume fills a real need."

Rev. Charles Dollen
The Priest

"Debra Hintz has provided a valuable tool for leaders who would like to present the local church's 'work at hand' as the work of the people of God."

Religious Education

Gathering Prayers

Debra Hintz

TWENTY-THIRD PUBLICATIONS
Mystic, Connecticut

ACKNOWLEDGMENTS

Scripture texts used in this work are taken from the *The Jerusalem Bible*, copyright © 1985, by Darton, Longman & Todd, Ltd. and Doubleday & Company, Inc. Used with permission of the publisher.

The Easter Sequence is taken from Joseph Connolly, *Hymns of the Roman Liturgy* (London: Longmans, Green, 1954).

The Pentecost Sequence is taken from the *Roman Missal* approved by the National Conference of Bishops of the United States, © 1964 by the National Catholic Welfare Conference, Inc.

Third Printing   1988

Twenty-Third Publications
185 Willow Street
P.O. Box 180
Mystic CT 06355
(203) 536-2611

ISBN 0-89622-296-9
Library of Congress Catalog Card Number 86-50239

Art by Debra Hintz

DEDICATED
to the future church.
May it be alive in the Spirit,
and filled with
compassion, courage, equality, and joy.

Contents

Introduction

Prayer binds us, unites us, and makes us one. As we gather in community, prayer gives us a common bond as we turn our attention to God and open ourselves to the presence and guidance of our Lord. We surrender ourselves to God's way, placing our trust in the One who is continuously with us, in us. Through prayer we are given the strength to do the will of the God who calls us.

This spirit is essential as we come together to share with one another, make decisions necessary for the growth of our community, reach out to those in need, and as we proclaim the gospel message. These prayer services provide the opportunity to begin our gatherings—be they meetings, study groups, planning groups, social events, or one of the many other occasions that bring us together as a Christian people — with time for worship so that the Spirit may permeate us through prayer and Scripture and bring us together as a community whose work is that of a God who cares.

A note on themes
The titles of the services are taken directly from the Scripture readings used and should give you a general idea of the themes of each service. It is recommended, however, that you read through an entire service to better familiarize yourself with the prayer.

Scripture readings
The texts of Scripture readings, except those read together by those who are assembled, are not included in the prayer services. The Word is more appropriately read from the book of Scriptures. A period of silence should be allowed after each of the readings to allow for reflection on the Word that has been proclaimed.

Intercessions
In most of the services the intercessions are spontaneous prayers. In response to the Word, those who have gathered are given the opportunity to express their needs as well as concerns beyond the local community. The responses to these prayers are not indicated and, thus, need to be chosen prior to beginning each service. An example: "Lord, hear our prayer," either recited or sung.

Music   Although songs are not indicated, you are encouraged to include music to enhance the services. Ideal times to do this are prior to or following the Call to Worship and at the conclusion of the service. You may also wish to sing a response to the Word and the intercessions.

Preparation   Those who lead prayer always need to prepare the service. Even though these services may be easy to follow, you need to be familiar with each one before praying. Music needs to be chosen, leaders and readers need to prepare their readings, and the environment needs to be set. All this should be done before the prayer service begins, so that all will enter into the experience and be touched by it.

Another key to a prayer service that flows is to prepare the people with any instructions before prayer begins. Make these as simple as possible, however. For example, if a psalm response is divided "left" and "right," let everyone know beforehand who is "left" and who is "right." Do not interrupt prayer to suddenly explain something. You may also want to explain or announce music selections beforehand.

It is also important to have a period of silence before a prayer service in order to allow the people to prepare, placing themselves in God's presence and setting their hearts and minds on prayer.

Setting   Even if you are coming together for a meeting, a special environment for prayer can still be achieved. Set a mood for prayer. Lights can be dimmed, a single candle lit, and background music played as people gather before prayer begins.

Creativity   When preparing a prayer service, use your creativity. The prayer will then become yours. If you feel you would like to use music where it is not indicated, do so. You might prefer to sing the psalm response. Or replace it with a song. Audiovisual materials can also be used. Slides, filmstrips, and movies can enhance prayer. Slides, for instance, can be used to illustrate a reading. A single slide projected during the entire prayer can help set a mood. Filmstrips and brief movies can be used in place of a reading. The use of light, water, oil, and other symbols can add another dimension to prayer.

God's Chosen Ones

CALL TO WORSHIP

Presider   Come, let us worship the Lord for he is our God and we are his people.
All   To you, O Lord, we give glory and praise.

Presider   Let us pray. Eternal God, we, your chosen people, gather in your presence. Always in need of your undying love and infinite wisdom, we reach out to you in prayer as we begin our time together. In this gathering we are reminded that it is you who call us together. Ever mindful of our call, we now pray.

THE WORD OF GOD

Reader   Romans 8:28-39

Response: Psalm 95

Reader   Come, let us cry out with joy to Yahweh.
All   Come, let us cry out with joy to Yahweh.

Reader   Come, let us cry out with joy to Yahweh.
acclaim the rock of our salvation.
Let us come into his presence with thanksgiving,
acclaim him with music.
All   Come, let us cry out with joy to Yahweh.

Reader   For Yahweh is a great God,
a king greater than all the gods.
In his power are the depths of the earth,
the peaks of the mountains are his;
the sea belongs to him, for he made it,
and the dry land, moulded by his hands.

All	Come, let us cry out with joy to Yahweh.
Reader	Come, let us bow low and do reverence; kneel before Yahweh who made us! For he is our God, and we the people of his sheepfold, the flock of his hand.
All	Come, let us cry out with joy to Yahweh.

INTERCESSIONS

Presider	Let us pray to the Lord our God who has chosen us to be his own. (Spontaneous Prayers)

THE LORD'S PRAYER

Presider	In the midst of this assembly, as a people called to be one in the Lord, let us together pray:
All	Our Father ....

CONCLUDING PRAYER

Presider	God of our mothers and fathers, you have made us a people all your own and have loved us with an everlasting love. To you we give thanks and praise and we sing of your great glory. Make your presence known to us in this gathering. We ask this in the name of our Lord Jesus Christ.
All	Amen.
Presider	Lord, bless and strengthen your people.
All	Let your face shine on us and bring us peace.

In Union With God And Our Lord Jesus Christ

CALL TO WORSHIP

Presider The Lord bless you.
All And give you peace.

Presider Praise be the God of all who has blessed us in Christ Jesus.
All He gathers his people again.

THE WORD OF GOD

Reader 1 John 1:1-4
Response: Psalm 138

Reader I thank you, Yahweh, with all my heart.
In the presence of angels I sing to you.
All I thank you, Yahweh, with all my heart.
In the presence of angels I sing to you.

Reader I thank you, Yahweh, with all my heart,
for you have listened to the cry I uttered.
In the presence of angels I sing to you,
I bow down before your holy Temple.
All I thank you, Yahweh....

Reader I praise your name for your faithful love and your constancy;
your promises surpass even your fame.
You heard me on the day when I called,
and you gave new strength to my heart.
All I thank you, Yahweh....

Reader All the kings of earth give thanks to you, Yahweh,
when they hear the promises you make;
they sing of Yahweh's ways,
'Great is the glory of Yahweh!'
Sublime as he is, Yahweh looks on the humble,
the proud he picks out from afar.
All I thank you, Yahweh....

Reader Though I live surrounded by trouble
you give me life—to my enemies' fury!
You stretch out your right hand and save me,
Yahweh will do all things for me.
Yahweh, your faithful love endures for ever,
do not abandon what you have made.
All I thank you, Yahweh....

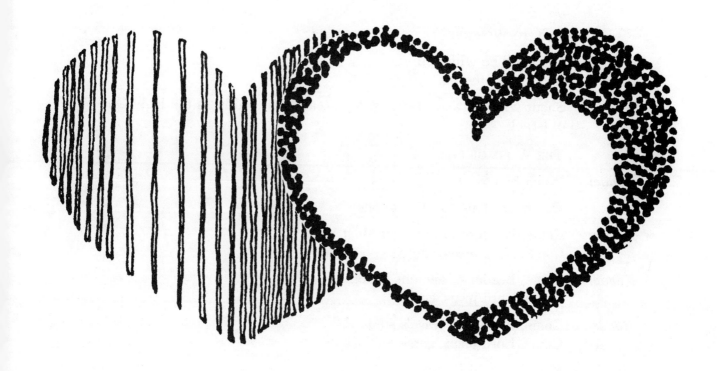

INTERCESSIONS

Presider   Let us pray to our God who hears our prayers and answers them. (Spontaneous Prayers)

PRAYER OF PRAISE

Reader   Chronicles 16:8-12, 15-17, 23-24, 35-36

CONCLUDING PRAYER

Presider   O Lord, you have gathered us together in fellowship with you and your Son, Jesus Christ. May the work we are about to begin reflect the word of life we have received that we may bear witness to it. We ask this in the name of our Lord Jesus Christ.

All   Amen.

Presider   May the Lord order our days in his peace,
hear our every prayer,
and lead us to everlasting life and joy.

All   Amen.

December 4, 1989

Come, Lord Jesus, Come

CALL TO WORSHIP

Presider   The Lord be with you.
All   And also with you.

Presider   Shout with joy and gladness, for great in our midst is the Holy One of Israel.

THE WORD OF GOD:

Reader   Isaiah 35:1-6, 10

Response: The "O" Antiphons

Reader   Come, Wisdom of our God Most High.
All   Come, Lord Jesus, come.

Reader   Come, Leader of ancient Israel.
All   Come, Lord Jesus, come.

Reader   Come, Flower of Jesse's stem.
All   Come, Lord Jesus, come.

Reader   Come, Key of David.
All   Come, Lord Jesus, come.

Reader   Come, Radiant Dawn.
All   Come, Lord Jesus, come.

Reader   Come, King of all nations.
All   Come, Lord Jesus, come.

Reader   Come, Emmanuel.
All   Come, Lord Jesus, come.

INTERCESSIONS

Presider   Let us pray to the Lord who ransom s us and brings us everlasting life. (Spontaneous Prayers)

CONCLUDING PRAYER

Presider   Lord God, source of our salvation, we await your coming when we will see your glory, the splendor of our God. Then will the eyes of the blind be opened and streams burst forth in the desert. Then will you ransom us and crown us with everlasting joy.

All   Glory to the Father, and to the Son, and to the Holy Spirit: As it was in the beginning, is now, and will be forever. Amen.

Justice and Peace Will Flourish

CALL TO WORSHIP

Presider   Our Lord is a God of justice. May God's peace and glory be with you all.
All   And also with you.

Presider   Lord, creator of the heavens and designer of the earth, we turn to you in this time of anticipation. As we proclaim you to be our God, increase our longing for Christ our Savior. Be with us as we prepare to see the glory of your kingdom.

THE WORD OF GOD

Reader   Isaiah 45:18-25

Response: Psalm 72

Reader   Justice shall flourish in his time,
    and fullness of peace for ever.
All   Justice shall flourish in his time,
    and fullness of peace for ever.

Reader   God, endow the king with your own fair judgement,
    the son of the king with your own saving justice,
that he may rule your people with justice,
    and your poor with fair judgement.
All   Justice shall flourish . . . .

Reader   In his days uprightness shall flourish,
    and peace in plenty till the moon is no more.
His empire shall stretch from sea to sea,
    from the river to the limits of the earth.
All   Justice shall flourish . . . .

Reader   For he rescues anyone needy who calls to him,
    and the poor who has no one to help.
He has pity on the weak and the needy,
    and saves the needy from death.
All   Justice shall flourish . . . .

Reader   May his name be blessed for ever,
    and endure in the sight of the sun.
In him shall be blessed every race in the world,
    and all nations call him blessed.
All   Justice shall flourish . . . .

INTERCESSIONS

Presider   Let us pray to our God who is gracious to those who cry out to him. (Spontaneous Prayers)

Presider   Gracious God, hear the prayers we commend to you and in your goodness answer them. We pray this in Jesus' name.

All   Amen.

PRAYER OF THANKSGIVING:

Reader   Isaiah 12

CONCLUDING PRAYER

Presider   Lord, our God, we await the coming of our Lord Jesus Christ who is our justice and peace. Strengthen our hearts that we may be ready to stand before him and proclaim to the world that you are indeed a God who saves. We ask this through Jesus Christ, our Savior and Brother.

All   Amen.

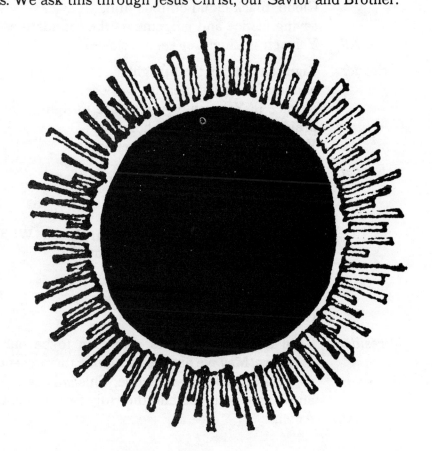

11

They Shall Call Him Emmanuel

CALL TO WORSHIP

Presider	Good news and great joy to all of the world.
All	This day is born our Savior, Christ the Lord.
Presider	Glory to God in heaven.
All	Peace to all people on earth.

THE WORD OF GOD

Reader	First Reading: Matthew 1:18-25

Response: Psalm 97

Reader	Yahweh is king! Let earth rejoice.
All	Yahweh is king! Let earth rejoice.
Reader	Yahweh is king! Let earth rejoice, the many isles be glad! Cloud, black cloud enfolds him, saving justice and judgements the foundations of his throne.
All	Yahweh is king! Let earth rejoice.
Reader	Light dawns for the upright, and joy for honest hearts. Rejoice in Yahweh, you who are upright, praise his unforgettable holiness.
All	Yahweh is king! Let earth rejoice.
Reader	Second Reading: Titus 2:11-14

PRAYERS OF PRAISE

Lord, you sent your Son to be our Savior. With great joy, we sing our praises to you. (Spontaneous Prayers)

Response: Glory to you, O Lord.

CONCLUDING PRAYER

Presider	Lord God, you gave us your Son to be our light in the midst of darkness. May we always recognize the presence of Christ in our lives as we await our blessed hope. This we ask in his name, he who lives and reigns with you and the Holy Spirit, one God, for ever and ever.
All	Amen.

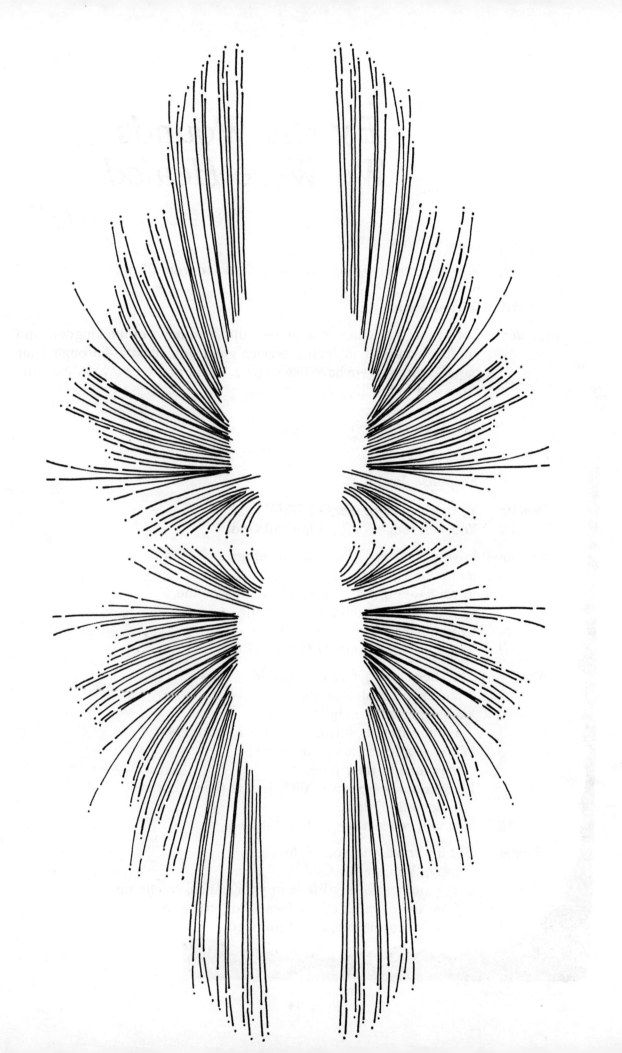

By His Wounds
We Were Healed

Presider   May grace, mercy and peace from God and from Christ Jesus our Lord be with you.

All   And also with you.

Presider   Lord Jesus, you came to announce the good news of the kingdom and emptied yourself in loving service even unto death. Through your paschal sacrifice we have been saved. Grant that we may embrace the cross and follow in your footsteps.

THE WORD OF GOD:

Reader   1 Peter 2:21-24

Response: Psalm 31

Reader   You will redeem me, O faithful God.

All   You will redeem me, O faithful God.

Reader   In you, Yahweh, I have taken refuge,
let me never be put to shame,
in your saving justice deliver me, rescue me,
to your hands I commit my spirit,
by you have I been redeemed.

All   You will redeem me, O faithful God.

Reader   The sheer number of my enemies
   makes me contemptible,
loathsome to my neighbours,
   and my friends shrink from me in horror.
When people see me in the street
   they take to their heels.
I have no more place in their hearts than a corpse,
   or something lost.

All   You will redeem me, O faithful God.

Reader   But my trust is in you, Yahweh;
   I say, 'You are my God,'
every moment of my life is in your hands, rescue me
   from the clutches of my foes who pursue me.

All   You will redeem me, O faithful God.

INTERCESSIONS

Presider   Let us pray to the God who saves us. (Spontaneous Prayers)

PRAYERS OF PRAISE

Presider   It was Christ who suffered that we may be saved. By his wounds we were healed and delivered from the snares of evil. To him we give glory as we pray:

You are a merciful Lord.
All   Glory to you, Lord Jesus Christ.

Presider   You take away the sins of the world.
All   Glory to you, Lord Jesus Christ.

Presider   You came to save us.
All   Glory to you, Lord Jesus Christ.

Presider   You were bound in cords.
All   Glory to you, Lord Jesus Christ.

Presider   You were whipped and scourged.
All   Glory to you, Lord Jesus Christ.

Presider   You were nailed to the cross.
All   Glory to you, Lord Jesus Christ.

Presider   You were buried and rose from the dead.
All   Glory to you, Lord Jesus Christ.

Presider   You ascended into heaven.
All   Glory to you, Lord Jesus Christ.

CONCLUDING PRAYER

Presider   May God who has called us to everlasting glory in Christ Jesus restore and strengthen us. May we accept in our own lives the mystery of the cross that we may be able to enter into the glory of his kingdom. We pray this in Jesus' name.
All   Amen.

Deliver Us By Your Wonders

CALL TO WORSHIP

Presider   The Lord be with you.
All   And also with you.

Presider   Lord, we are a stubborn people who turn from you and reject your word. Yet you wait for us to return for you are a God of justice. Hear us now as we pray for your kindness and mercy so that we may be reconciled once again during this season of penitence. Be with us as we prepare to celebrate the resurrection and glory of our Lord Jesus Christ. We pray this in his name.
All   Amen.

THE WORD OF GOD:

Reader   Isaiah 30:~~12-18~~ 1 through 22 *(verses)*

         Response: ~~Daniel 3:26-29, 41-43~~ 1 Peter chp 2 verse 1, 11

Reader   Rescue us in accordance with your wonderful deeds
and win fresh glory for your name, O Lord.
All   Rescue us in accordance with your wonderful deeds
and win fresh glory for your name, O Lord.

Reader   May you be blessed and revered, Lord, God of our ancestors,
may your name be held glorious for ever.
For you are upright in all that you have done for us,
all your deeds are true,
all your ways right,
all your judgements true.
All   Rescue us . . . .

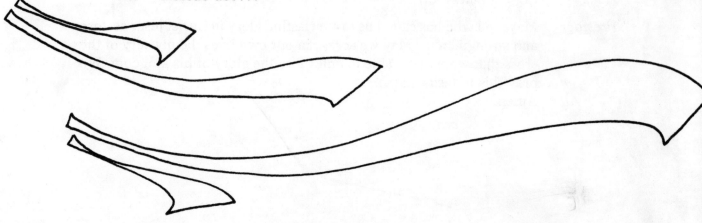

16

Reader　True is the sentence you have given
in all that you have brought down on us
and on Jerusalem, the holy city of our ancestors,
for you have treated us rightly and truly,
as our sins deserve.

All　Rescue us ....

Reader　And now we put our whole heart into following you,
into fearing you and seeking your face once more.
Do not abandon us to shame
but treat us in accordance with your gentleness,
in accordance with the greatness of your mercy.
Rescue us in accordance with your wonderful deeds
and win fresh glory for your name, O Lord.

All　Rescue us ....

INTERCESSIONS

Presider　Lord, hear us as we pray for your kindness and great mercy.
(Spontaneous Prayers)

CONCLUDING PRAYER

Presider　Almighty and merciful God, you never abandon your children, but wait patiently for us to turn to you that you might show us favor. Break through our stubbornness and the hardness of our hearts and minds so that we may be reconciled to you. In our desire for conversion, we pray this through our Lord Jesus Christ who lives and reigns with you and the Holy Spirit, one God, for ever and ever.

All　Amen.

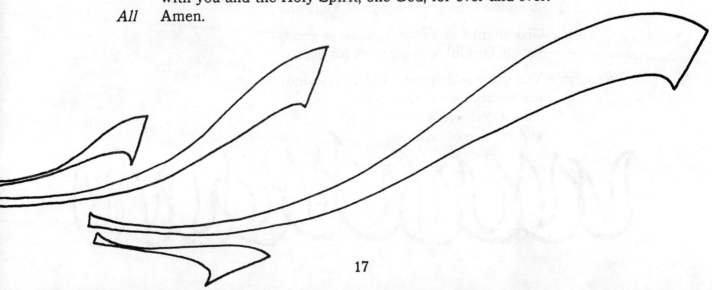

Christ Our Hope Has Risen

CALL TO WORSHIP

Presider May grace and peace from God and from Christ Jesus our Savior be with you.

All And also with you.

Presider Blessed by our God who has raised up the Lord Jesus.

All To you be praise, honor and glory now and for ever. Amen. Alleluia!

THE WORD OF GOD

Reader Mark 16:1-8

Response: Psalm 118

Reader Give thanks to Yahweh for he is good,
for his faithful love endures for ever.

All Give thanks to Yahweh for he is good,
for his faithful love endures for ever.

Reader Give thanks to Yahweh for he is good,
for his faithful love endures for ever.
Let the House of Israel say,
'His faithful love endures for ever.'

All Give thanks to Yahweh for he is good,
for his faithful love endures for ever.

Reader 'Yahweh's right hand is triumphant,
Yahweh's right hand is victorious,
Yahweh's right hand is triumphant!'
I shall not die, I shall live
to recount the great deeds of Yahweh.

All Give thanks to Yahweh for he is good,
for his faithful love endures for ever.

Reader The stone which the builders rejected
has become the cornerstone;
This is Yahweh's doing,
and we marvel at it.

All   Give thanks to Yahweh for he is good,
for his faithful love endures for ever.

EASTER SEQUENCE

Reader   To the Paschal Victim let Christians offer a sacrifice of praise.

The Lamb redeemed the sheep. Christ, sinless, reconciled sinners to the Father.

Death and life were locked together in a unique struggle. Life's captain died; now he reigns, never more to die.

Tell us, Mary, "What did you see on the way?"

"I saw the tomb of the now living Christ. I saw the glory of Christ, now risen.

I saw angels who gave witness; the cloths too which once had covered head and limbs.

Christ my hope has arisen. He will go before his own into Galilee."

We know that Christ had indeed risen from the dead. Do you, conqueror and king, have mercy on us. Amen. Alleluia.

INTERCESSIONS

Presider   Lord, in your great goodness salvation became ours in the death and resurrection of your Son. Hear us now as we pray.
(Spontaneous Prayers)

CONCLUDING PRAYER

Presider   All-powerful and ever-living God, we praise you with great joy as we celebrate your redemptive work. Christ, who took away the sins of the world, destroyed our death through his dying and in his rising has restored our life. Blessed are you who has raised up the Lord Jesus; you who will raise us in our turn and put us by his side.

All   Glory to the Father, and to the Son, and to the Holy Spirit: As it was in the beginning, is now, and will be forever. Amen.

Receive the Holy Spirit

CALL TO WORSHIP

Presider   The grace of our Lord Jesus Christ and the love of God and the fellowship of the Holy Spirit be with you.

All   And also with you.

Presider   Let us pray. O God, send down upon us your Spirit to enlighten the minds of the faithful. Let that Spirit continue to work in the world through the hearts of those who believe. Graced with the gifts the Spirit brings, may we confess that Jesus Christ is Lord who lives and reigns with you and the Holy Spirit, one God, for ever and ever.

All   Amen.

THE WORD OF GOD

Reader   John 20:19-23

PENTECOST SEQUENCE

Reader   Come, Holy Spirit, come!
And from your celestial home
  Shed a ray of light divine!

Come, Father of the poor!
Come, source of all our store!
  Come, within our bosoms shine!

You, of comforters the best;
You, the soul's most welcome guest;
  Sweet refreshment here below;

In our labor, rest most sweet;
Grateful coolness in the heat;
  Solace in the midst of woe.

O most blessed Light divine,
Shine within these hearts of yours,
  And our inmost being fill!

Where you are not, man has naught,
Nothing good in deed or thought,
  Nothing free from taint of ill.

Heal our wounds, our strength renew;
On our dryness pour your dew;
  Wash the stains of guilt away;

Bend the stubborn heart and will;
Melt the frozen, warm the chill;
   Guide the steps that go astray.

On the faithful, who adore
And confess you, evermore
   In your sev'nfold gift descend;

Give them virtue's sure reward;
Give them your salvation, Lord;
   Give them joys that never end.

Amen. Alleluia.

INTERCESSIONS

Presider   Lord, to you we offer our prayers of petition. Hear us as we pray for the presence of the Spirit among us. (Spontaneous Prayers)

CONCLUDING PRAYER

Presider   Listen, O God, to your people united in prayer. Continually pour forth upon your church the gift of your Spirit to breathe upon our hearts and minds so that strenghtened we may bring the message to all that Jesus is Lord. Grant this in his name.

All   Amen.

Presider   Let us go forth in peace, rejoicing in the power of the Holy Spirit.
All   Thanks be to God who sends us forth.

I Serve You
In the Midst of Your People

CALL TO WORSHIP

Presider   Grace and peace be yours from our gracious God and from the Lord Jesus Christ!

All   And also yours.

Presider   Let us pray. Lord God, you have called us to serve you in the midst of your people. We pray that we may serve with understanding hearts that we may know what is right. Trusting in your guidance, we reach out to you with our talents and our inadequacies. Strengthen us that we may do your will. For this we pray in the name of our Lord Jesus Christ.

All   Amen.

THE WORD OF GOD

Reader   1 Kings 3:7-15

INTERCESSIONS

Presider   Lord, our needs are many. Hear us as we pray. (Spontaneous Prayers)

THE LORD'S PRAYER

Presider   Gathering our prayers into one, let us together pray:

All   Our Father in heaven,
may your name be held holy,
your kingdom come,
your will be done
on earth as in heaven.
Give us today our daily bread.
And forgive us our debts,
as we have forgiven those who are in debt to us.
And do not put us to the test,
but save us from the evil one.

CONCLUDING PRAYER

Presider   Lord, you are a generous God. Gift us with wisdom and understanding so that our ministries may accomplish the work of Jesus Christ. Let your spirit fill our lives; let your love make us compassionate servants. We ask this in the name of our Lord Jesus Christ, who taught us to be servants of all.

All   Amen.

Ministers of God

CALL TO WORSHIP

Presider   The favor of the Lord Jesus be with you.
All   And also with you.

THE WORD OF GOD

Reader   First Reading: 2 Corinthians 6:1-10

Response: Psalm 113

Reader   Blessed be the name of Yahweh henceforth and for ever.
All   Blessed be the name of Yahweh henceforth and for ever.

Reader   Praise, servants of Yahweh,
praise the name of Yahweh.
Blessed be the name of Yahweh,
henceforth and for ever.
All   Blessed be the name....

Reader   From the rising of the sun to its setting,
praised be the name of Yahweh!
Supreme over all nations is Yahweh,
supreme over the heavens his glory.
All   Blessed be the name....

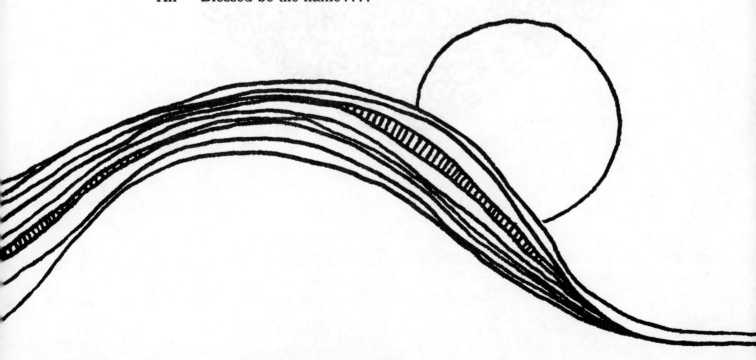

Reader	Supreme over all nations is Yahweh, supreme over the heavens his glory. Who is like Yahweh our God?
All	Blessed be the name....
Reader	He raises the poor from the dust, he lifts the needy from the dunghill, to give them a place among princes, among princes of his people. He lets the barren woman be seated at home, the happy mother of sons.
All	Blessed be the name....
Reader	Second Reading: John 13:12-17

INTERCESSIONS

Presider	Lord, God, you call us to be servants who imitate Christ. Hear now the prayers of your people. (Spontaneous Prayers)

THE LORD'S PRAYER

Presider	Let us offer the prayer our Lord Jesus Christ taught us:
All	Our Father in heaven, may your name be held holy, your kingdom come, your will be done on earth as in heaven. Give us today our daily bread. And forgive us our debts, as we have forgiven those who are in debt to us. And do not put us to the test, but save us from the evil one.

CONCLUDING PRAYER

Presider	May God and the Lord Jesus Christ grant us peace and love and faith.
All	Grace be with all who love our Lord Jesus Christ with unfailing love.

Speak, Lord
Your Servant Listens

CALL TO WORSHIP

Presider   The grace and peace of the Lord Jesus Christ be with you.
All   And also with you.

Presider   Let us pray. Lord God, we your servants gather in your presence to be strengthened and healed, inspired and empowered so that our work may make known your compassion. Speak to us so that we may be a community that celebrates and proclaims your redemptive work. May we be ever faithful to our call, always acting with determination and conviction. We ask this in the name of Jesus Christ, our Lord and Brother.
All   Amen.

THE WORD OF GOD

Reader   1 Samuel 3:3-10, 19

INTERCESSIONS

Presider   Let us pray to the Lord our God who hears our needs and answers them. (Spontaneous Prayers)

THE LORD'S PRAYER

Gathering our prayers and praises into one, let us together pray the prayer that Jesus taught us.
All   Our Father . . . .

CONCLUDING PRAYER

Presider   Lord God, hear the prayers of your people. Accept our work and our words as a sign of our great love for you. Forgive us for the times we falter and give us strength in return. Be with us always as you were with Samuel so that all we do may be a powerful witness to all the world. We pray this in the name of our Lord Jesus Christ who lives and reigns with you and the Holy Spirit, one God for ever and ever.
All   Amen.

Love Justice

CALL TO WORSHIP

Presider   May grace and peace from God and from the Lord Jesus Christ be with you all.

All   And also with you.

Presider   As we come together in prayer, let us open our hearts and minds to the Word of God and ask for the wisdom and strength we may need to respond as followers of Christ Jesus, our Lord.

THE WORD OF GOD

Reader   Wisdom 1:1-15

Response: Psalm 1

Reader   How blessed is anyone who rejects the advice of the wicked
but delights in the law of Yahweh.

All   How blessed is anyone who rejects the advice of the wicked
but delights in the law of Yahweh.

Reader   How blessed is anyone who rejects the advice of the wicked
and does not take a stand in the path that sinners tread,
nor a seat in company with cynics,
but who delights in the law of Yahweh
and murmurs his law day and night.

All   How blessed . . . .

Reader   Such a one is like a tree planted near streams;
it bears fruit in season
and its leaves never wither,
and every project succeeds.
How different the wicked, how different!

All   How blessed . . . .

Reader   Just like chaff blown around by the wind
the wicked will not stand firm at the Judgement
nor sinners in the gathering of the upright.
For Yahweh watches over the path of the upright,
but the path of the wicked is doomed.

All   How blessed . . . .

INTERCESSIONS

Presider   Gracious God, we call upon you for we are in need of your guidance as we work to bring justice to all. Hear our prayers and answer them. (Spontaneous Prayers)

CONCLUDING PRAYER

Presider   God, our Creator, you who fashioned us in your own image and likeness, we are ever grateful for the spirit of justice with which you rule. We pray that we, too, may make that justice known to all. May we be always disciplined in our acts and ever faithful in our words. We ask this through our Lord Jesus Christ, your Son, he lives and reigns with you and the Holy Spirit, one God for ever and ever.

All   Amen.

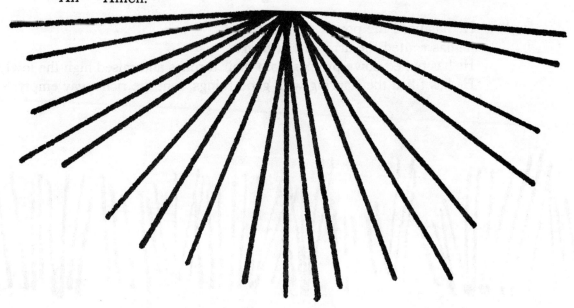

Share Your Bread With the Hungry

CALL TO WORSHIP

Presider   May grace, mercy and peace from God and from Christ Jesus our Lord be with you.

All   And also with you.

Presider   Let us pray. Lord God, we are ever mindful of those subjected to the injustices of the world. Hear us now as we pray for your presence among us as we work to remove oppression from our midst. We ask this in the name of our Lord Jesus Christ.

All   Amen.

THE WORD OF GOD

Reader   Isaiah 58:6-11

CANTICLE OF MARY

Right   My soul proclaims the greatness of the Lord
and my spirit rejoices in God my Saviour;
because he has looked upon the humiliation of his servant.

Left   Yes, from now onwards all generations will call me blessed,
for the Almighty has done great things for me.
Holy is his name,
and his faithful love extends age after age to those who fear him.

Right   He has used the power of his arm,
he has routed the arrogant of heart.
He has pulled down princes from their thrones and raised high the lowly.
He has filled the starving with good things, sent the rich away empty.

Left   He has come to the help of Israel his servant, mindful of his faithful love
—according to the promise he made to our ancestors—
of his mercy to Abraham and to his descendants for ever.

INTERCESSIONS

Presider   Lord God, hear the prayers of your people as we reach out to you in
need. (Spontaneous Prayers)

THE LORD'S PRAYER

Presider   Let us pray as Jesus did:
All   Our Father in heaven,
may your name be held holy,
your kingdom come,
your will be done
on earth as in heaven.
Give us today our daily bread.
And forgive us our debts,
as we have forgiven those who are in debt to us.
And do not put us to the test,
but save us from the evil one.

CONCLUDING PRAYER

Presider   Lord God of power and might, direct our concerns to the poor and
oppressed of the world. Let us hear in their voices their hopes and
their struggles that we may respond in an effort to restore their
human dignity. May we find within ourselves the conviction to always
put the powerless foremost in our hearts and minds that all may know
you are a God who cares. Grant this through Christ out Lord.
All   Amen.

They Shall Beat Their Swords Into Plowshares

CALL TO WORSHIP

Presider   May mercy and peace from God and Christ Jesus our Savior be with you.
All   And also with you.

Presider   Lord, we ask for peace throughout our world. Make your love and wisdom known to all so that all people may put aside the selfish ways which lead to conflict. Hear us now as we pray for your presence among us and all nations.

THE WORD OF GOD

Reader   Canticle: Isaiah 2:2-5

Reader   House of Jacob, come, let us walk in Yahweh's light.
All   House of Jacob, come, let us walk in Yahweh's light.

Reader   It will happen in the final days
that the mountain of Yahweh's house
will rise higher than the mountains
and tower above the heights.
Then all the nations will stream to it.
All   House of Jacob, come, let us walk in Yahweh's light.

Reader   Many peoples will come to it and say,
'Come, let us go up to the mountain of Yahweh,
to the house of the God of Jacob
that he may teach us his ways
so that we may walk in his paths.'
For the Law will issue from Zion
and the word of Yahweh from Jerusalem.
All   House of Jacob, come, let us walk in Yahweh's light.

Reader   Then he will judge between the nations
and arbitrate between many peoples.
They will hammer their swords into ploughshares
and their spears into sickles.
Nation will not lift sword against nation,

no longer will they learn how to make war.

All   House of Jacob, come, let us walk in Yahweh's light.

Reader   Reading: John 14:23-29

INTERCESSIONS

Presider   Lord God, hear our prayers for peace and your presence among us.
(Spontaneous Prayers)

PRAYER OF ST. FRANCIS

Presider   Together let us pray:

All   Lord, make me an instrument of your peace.
Where there is hatred, let me sow love;
    where there is injury, pardon;
    where there is doubt, faith;
    where there is despair, hope;
    where there is darkness, light; and
    where there is sadness, joy.

O divine Master, grant that I may not so much seek
    to be consoled as to console,
    to be understood as to understand,
    to be loved as to love.
For it is in giving that we receive,
    it is in pardoning that we are pardoned; and
    it is in dying that we are born to eternal life.

CONCLUDING PRAYER

Presider   God of peace, you sent your Son as a gift of salvation, a gift of peace.
He prayed that we not be distressed or fearful as we carry out that
which you have commanded us to do. As we work for peace in this
world, be with us so that we do not falter or yield to the ways of evil.
We ask this in the name of Jesus Christ, the prince of peace.

All   Amen.

Though I Am Afflicted And Poor

CALL TO WORSHIP

Presider May our God and our Lord Jesus Christ grant you peace and love and faith.

All Grace be with all who love our Lord Jesus Christ with unfailing love.

Presider Let us pray. Lord God, your love is always present and all-embracing. Your faithfulness and kindness reach out to all as you especially remember the poor of the world. We pray that we may learn to imitate you in bringing hope to the oppressed. May your example of unconditional love motivate us to be among the poor and afflicted so that they may know your justice. We ask this through Christ our Lord.

All Amen.

THE WORD OF GOD

Reader First Reading: Deuteronomy 24:17-22

Response: Psalm 40

Reader I proclaim the saving justice of Yahweh.
All I proclaim the saving justice of Yahweh.

Reader I waited, I waited for Yahweh,
    then he stooped to me
    and heard my cry for help.
He put a fresh song in my mouth,
    praise of our God.

All I proclaim the saving justice of Yahweh.

Reader In the scroll of the book it is written of me,
    my delight is to do your will;
your law, my God,
    is deep in my heart.

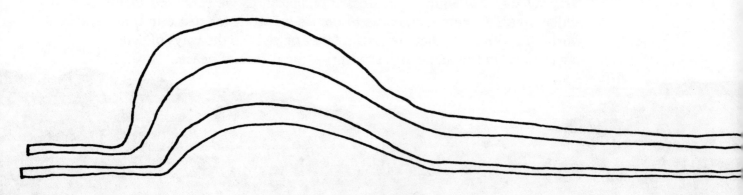

All   I proclaim the saving justice of Yahweh.

Reader   I proclaim the saving justice of Yahweh
        in the great assembly.
See, I will not hold my tongue,
        as you well know.
I have not kept your saving justice
        locked in the depths of my heart,
        but have spoken of your constancy and saving help.

All   I proclaim the saving justice of Yahweh.

Reader   Poor and needy as I am,
        the Lord has me in mind.
You, my helper, my Saviour,
        my God, do not delay.

All   I proclaim the saving justice of Yahweh.

Second Reading: Hebrews 13:1-3, 14-16

INTERCESSIONS

Presider   Loving Creator, hear the prayers of your people as we reach out to you. (Spontaneous Prayers)

CONCLUDING PRAYER

Presider   Lord, we are a people who need to be reminded to extend our hospitality to those in need. When in our humanness we neglect the poor and afflicted of the world, impel us to reach out to them and offer support and love. Help us to help them rise above their situations as we work to alleviate the circumstances that cause the oppressive conditions so prevalent in our world. Grant this through Christ our Lord.

All   Amen.

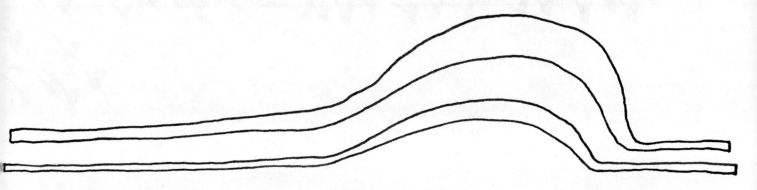

Forgiveness
From the Heart

Presider May grace, mercy and peace from God and Christ Jesus our Lord be with you.

All And also with you.

THE WORD OF GOD

Reader First Reading: James 5:16-20

Response: Psalm 51

Right Have mercy on me, O God, in your faithful love,
in your great tenderness wipe away my offences;
wash me thoroughly from my guilt,
purify me from my sin.

Left For I am well aware of my offences,
my sin is constantly in mind.
Against you, you alone, I have sinned,
I have done what you see to be wrong,

Right God, create in me a clean heart,
renew within me a resolute spirit,
do not thrust me away from your presence,
do not take away from me your spirit of holiness.

Left   Give me back the joy of your salvation,
sustain in me a generous spirit.
I shall teach the wicked your paths,
and sinners will return to you.

Reader   Second Reading: Matthew 18:21-35

INTERCESSIONS

Presider   Let us pray to the Lord our God who continues to bless us with his mercy and love. (Spontaneous Prayers)

THE LORD'S PRAYER

Presider   Let us pray as Jesus did:
All   Our Father . . . .

CONCLUDING PRAYER

Presider   God of peace, make us perfect and holy; keep us safe and blameless, spirit, soul and body, for the coming of our Lord. We ask this through our Lord Jesus Christ, your Son, who lives and reigns with you and the Holy Spirit, one God, for ever and ever.
All   Amen.

I Will Cleanse You

CALL TO WORSHIP

Presider   Grace and peace to you from God our creator and our Lord Jesus Christ.
All   And also to you.

Presider   Let us pray. Gracious God, hear us as we ask for your forgiveness and compassion. In times of weakness we have strayed from your light. With sorrow we pray that you cleanse us from all our impurities. We ask this through our Lord Jesus Christ, your Son, who lives and reigns with you and the Holy Spirit, one God, for ever and ever.
All   Amen.

THE WORD OF GOD

Reader   Canticle: Ezekiel 36:24-28

Reader   For I shall take you from among the nations and gather you back from all the countries, and bring you home to your own country.
All   Lord, have mercy on me.

Reader   I shall pour clean water over you and you will be cleansed; I shall cleanse you of all your filth and of all your foul idols.
All   Lord, have mercy on me.

Reader   I shall give you a new heart, and put a new spirit in you; I shall remove the heart of stone from your bodies and give you a heart of flesh instead.
All   Lord, have mercy on me.

Reader   I shall put my spirit in you, and make you keep my laws, and respect and practise my judgements.
All   Lord, have mercy on me.

Reader   You will live in the country which I gave your ancestors. You will be

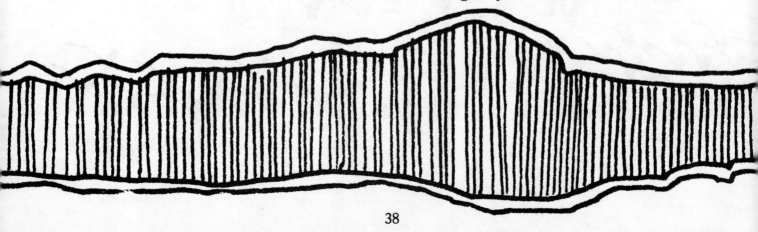

my people and I shall be your God.

All Lord, have mercy on me.

Reader Reading: 1 John 1:5-2:2

INTERCESSIONS

Presider Let us pray to the Lord our God who hears our prayers and answers us. (Spontaneous Prayers)

THE LORD'S PRAYER

Presider Gathering our prayers into one, let us confidently pray:
All Our Father in heaven,
may your name be held holy,
your kingdom come,
your will be done
on earth as in heaven.
Give us today our daily bread.
And forgive us our debts,
as we have forgiven those who are in debt to us.
And do not put us to the test,
but save us from the evil one.

CONCLUDING PRAYER

Presider God of our fathers and mothers, you have sent Jesus Christ as an offering for our sins. It is in him we have been cleansed from every wrong. As we acknowledge the evil in our lives, give us a new heart and place a new spirit within us, for then we will be known as your people, as children of the light. For this we pray through Jesus, our Lord and brother.
All Amen.

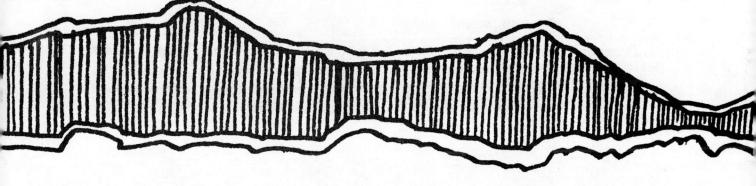

I Will Remember
Their Sin No More

CALL TO WORSHIP

Presider   The grace of our Lord Jesus Christ and the love of God and the fellowship of the Holy Spirit be with you all.

All   And also with you.

PENITENTIAL RITE

Presider   Let us pray. Lord God of endless mercy, look upon your people and bring us your compassion and peace. Let us be reconciled once again as we pray:
Lord, we have sinned against you.

All   Lord, have mercy.

Presider   Lord, show us your mercy and your compassion.

All   And grant us your salvation.

Presider   May our God of endless mercy have mercy on us and forgive us our sins that we may obtain everlasting life.

All   Amen.

THE WORD OF GOD

Reader   Jeremiah 31:31-34

INTERCESSIONS

Presider   Almighty God, we pray for your mercy and love. (Spontaneous Prayers)

THE LORD'S PRAYER

Presider   Let us together pray for forgiveness and guidance with the words of Jesus Christ:

All   Our Father....

CONCLUDING PRAYER

Presider   Lord, you are indeed a God who saves us. You have placed your law within us and written it upon our hearts. We reach out to you that we may be strong in the midst of temptation and always faithful to your ways. We pray this in the name of Jesus Christ our Lord.

All   Amen.

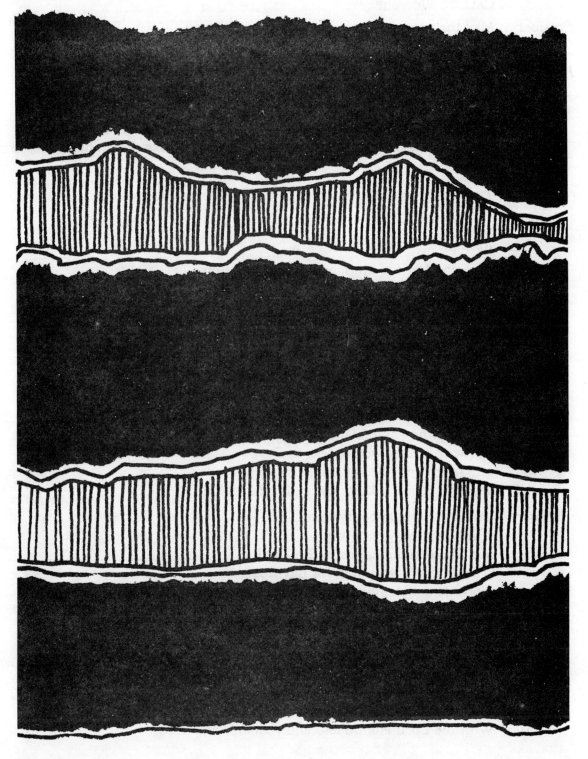

With You Is Forgiveness

CALL TO WORSHIP

Presider   May the peace and mercy of God be with you.

All   And also with you.

Presider   Let us pray. Almighty and merciful God, you sent Christ Jesus into the world to save sinners. Your mercy and grace you grant in overflowing measure. Open our eyes, our hearts and our minds that we may know the evil in our lives. Cleanse us and make us strong so that we might reflect the image of your Son. We ask this in his name.

All   Amen.

THE WORD OF GOD

Reader   1 Timothy 1:12-17

Response: Psalm 130

Reader   With the Lord is kindness and redemption.

All   With the Lord is kindness and redemption.

Reader   From the depths I call to you, Yahweh:
     Lord, hear my cry.
Listen attentively
     to the sound of my pleading!

All   With the Lord is kindness and redemption.

Reader   If you kept a record of our sins,
     Lord, who could stand their ground?
But with you is forgiveness
     that you may be revered.

All   With the Lord is kindness and redemption.

Reader   I rely, my whole being relies,
     Yahweh, on your promise.
My whole being hopes in the Lord,
     more than watchmen for daybreak;
more than watchmen for daybreak
     let Israel hope in Yahweh.

All   With the Lord is kindness and redemption.

Reader   For with Yahweh is faithful love,
     with him generous ransom;
and he will ransom Israel
     from all its sins.

All   With the Lord is kindness and redemption.

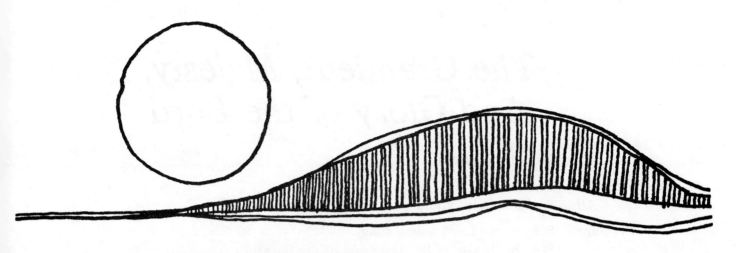

EXAMINATION OF CONSCIENCE

Presider   In silence, let us call to mind the times we have turned from the love of our God.

CONFITEOR

Presider   Let us together repent for our sins:

All   I confess to almighty God,
and to you, my brothers and sisters,
that I have sinned through my own fault
in my thoughts and in my words,
in what I have done,
and in what I have failed to do;
and I ask blessed Mary, ever virgin,
all the angels and saints,
and you my brothers and sisters,
to pray for me to the Lord our God.

Presider   Lord Jesus, you came to save us sinners. Lord, have mercy.
All   Lord, have mercy.

Presider   Lord Jesus, you grant your mercy in overflowing measure. Christ, have mercy.
All   Christ, have mercy.

Presider   Lord Jesus, to you be honor and glory forever. Lord, have mercy.
All   Lord, have mercy.

CONCLUDING PRAYER

Presider   Lord, we are ever grateful for your compassion and mercy. Renew in us a spirit of love; transform us into a people whose lives are reflections of our Lord Jesus Christ. As we give you thanks for the mercy you have shown, we sing your praise saying: Glory to you through Christ in the Holy Spirit, now and forever.
All   Amen.

The Grandeur, Majesty, And Glory of the Lord

CALL TO WORSHIP

Presider The Lord be with you.
All And also with you.

Presider Sing to the Lord a new song.
Sing his praise in the assembly of the faithful.

THE WORD OF GOD

Reader 1 Chronicles 29:10-13

PRAYER OF PRAISE AND THANKSGIVING

Presider Lord God, creator of heaven and earth, you have done wondrous things for us. Hear us as we proclaim your praise and give you thanks. (Spontaneous Prayers)

Response: Lord, we give you thanks and praise.

BLESSING PRAYER

Reader Sirach 50:22-24

Presider Let us pray together:
All And now bless the God of all things,
  the doer of great deeds everywhere,
who has exalted our days from the womb
  and has acted mercifully towards us.
May he grant us cheerful hearts
  and bring peace in our time,
  in Israel for ages on ages.
May his mercy be faithfully with us,
  may he redeem us in our own times!

CONCLUDING PRAYER

Presider And may the peace and glory of God which is beyond all understanding keep our hearts and minds in the knowledge and love of God and his Son our Lord Jesus Christ.
All Amen.

The Glory to Be Revealed

CALL TO WORSHIP

Presider   Praise the LORD, all you nations;
         glorify him, all you peoples!

All   For steadfast is his kindness toward us, and the fidelity of the LORD
         endures forever.

THE WORD OF GOD

Reader   Romans 8:18-27

CANTICLE OF ZECHARIAH

Right   Blessed be the Lord, the God of Israel,
         for he has visited his people, he has set them free,
         and he has established for us a saving power
         in the House of his servant David,

Left   just as he proclaimed,
         by the mouth of his holy prophets from ancient times,
         that he would save us from our enemies
         and from the hands of all those who hate us
         and show faithful love to our ancestors,
         and so keep in mind his holy covenant.

Right   This was the oath he swore
         to our father Abraham,
         that he would grant us, free from fear,
         to be delivered from the hands of our enemies,
         to serve him in holiness and uprightness
         in his presence, all our days.

Left   And you, little child,
         you shall be called Prophet of the Most High,
         for you will go before the Lord
         to prepare a way for him,
         to give his people knowledge of salvation
         through the forgiveness of their sins,

Right   because of the faithful love of our God
         in which the rising Sun has come from on high to visit us,
         to give light to those who live

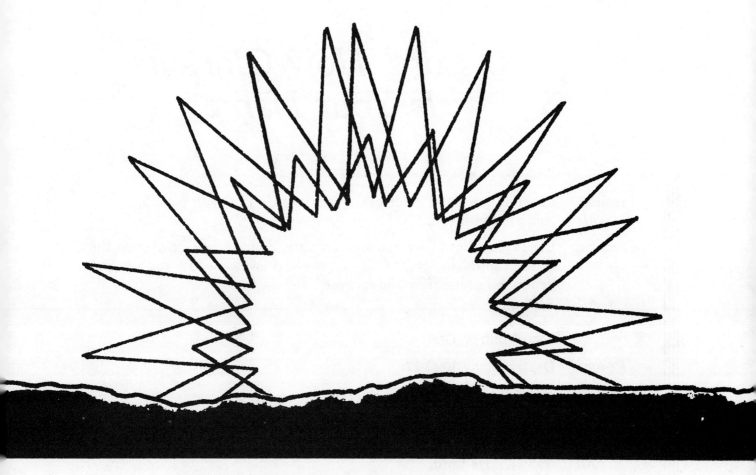

in darkness and the shadow dark as death,
and to guide our feet
into the way of peace.

INTERCESSIONS

Presider   Let us pray to the Lord our God. (Spontaneous Prayers)

THE LORD'S PRAYER

Presider   With longing for the coming of God's kingdom, let us pray as Jesus did:

   All   Our Father . . . .

CONCLUDING PRAYER

Presider   Lord God, you send your Spirit to bring us hope and help us in our weakness as we await the coming of your glorious kingdom. May all creation be ever faithful to you as we look to the day when that glory will be revealed in us. It is in faith we lift our voices and together pray:

   All   Glory to the Father, and to the Son,
and to the Holy Spirit:
As it was in the beginning, is now,
and will be forever. Amen.

O Lord, How Glorious Is Your Name

CALL TO WORSHIP

Presider   May the peace and grace of our glorious God be with you all.

All   And also with you.

Presider   Let us pray. Lord God, you are our glory. You are the God of gods, the Lord of lords, the great God, mighty and awesome. To you we give honor and praise now and forever.

All   Amen.

THE WORD OF GOD

Reader   Deuteronomy 10:12-22

Response: Psalm 8

Reader   Yahweh our Lord,
how majestic is your name throughout the world!

All   Yahweh our Lord,
how majestic is your name throughout the world!

Reader   Yahweh our Lord,
how majestic is your name throughout the world!
Whoever keeps singing of your majesty higher than the heavens,
even through the mouths of children, or of babes in arms,
you make him a fortress, firm against your foes,
to subdue the enemy and the rebel.

All   Yahweh our Lord,
how majestic is your name throughout the world!

Reader   I look up at your heavens, shaped by your fingers,
at the moon and the stars you set firm—
what are human beings that you spare a thought for them,
or the child of Adam that you care for him?

All   Yahweh our Lord,
how majestic is your name throughout the world!

Reader   Yet you have made him little less than a god,
you have crowned him with glory and beauty,
made him lord of the works of your hands,
put all things under his feet.

48

All   Yahweh our Lord,
how majestic is your name throughout the world!

INTERCESSIONS

Presider   Let us pray to the Lord our God. (Spontaneous Prayers)

Presider   Lord, hear the prayers we have commended to you. It is with confidence we bring them before you that you may grant them in the name of our Lord Jesus Christ.

All   Amen.

GLORIA

Presider   Let us give glory to God:

All   Glory to God in the highest,
    and peace to his people on earth.
Lord, God, heavenly King.
almighty God and Father,
we worship you, we give you thanks,
    we praise you for your glory.
Lord Jesus Christ, only Son of the Father,
Lord God, Lamb of God,
you take away the sin of the world:
    have mercy on us;
you are seated at the right hand of the Father:
    receive our prayer.
For you alone are the Holy One,
you alone are the Lord,
you alone are the Most High,
    Jesus Christ.
    with the Holy Spirit,
    in the glory of God the Father.
    Amen.

CONCLUDING PRAYER

Presider   Blessed are you, Lord our God, and blessed is your glorious name.

All   Glory to the Father, and to the Son, and to the Holy Spirit: As it was in the beginning, is now, and will be forever. Amen.

Through Christ
We Are Redeemed

CALL TO WORSHIP

Presider   Grace and peace be yours from God and the Lord Jesus Christ!
   All   And also yours.

Presider   Let us pray. Lord God, you have bestowed on us every spiritual blessing in heaven. You have chosen us to be your own. Hear us as we give you praise now and for ever.
   All   Amen.

THE WORD OF GOD

Reader   Ephesians 1:3-10

   Response: Psalm 98:1-6

Reader   Sing a new song to Yahweh,
for he has performed wonders.
   All   Sing a new song to Yahweh,
for he has performed wonders.

Reader   Sing a new song to Yahweh,
for he has performed wonders,
his saving power is in his right hand
and his holy arm.
Yahweh has made known his saving power,
revealed his saving justice for the nations to see,
mindful of his faithful love and his constancy
to the House of Israel.
   All   Sing a new song to Yahweh.
for he has performed wonders.

Reader   Let the sea thunder, and all that it holds,
the world and all who live in it.
Let the rivers clap their hands,
and the mountains shout for joy together,
at Yahweh's approach, for he is coming to judge the earth;
he will judge the world with saving justice
and the nations with fairness.
   All   Sing a new song to Yahweh,
for he has performed wonders.

Reader   The whole wide world has seen
the saving power of our God.

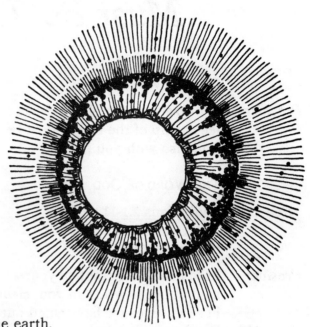

Acclaim Yahweh, all the earth,
burst into shouts of joy!
Play to Yahweh on the harp,
to the sound of instruments;
to the sound of trumpet and horn,
acclaim the presence of the King.

All Sing a new song to Yahweh,
for he has performed wonders.

INTERCESSIONS

Presider Let us pray to our God, the father of our Lord Jesus Christ.
(Spontaneous Prayers)

THE LORD'S PRAYER

Presider Gathering our prayers into one, let us pray:
All Our Father . . . .

CONCLUDING PRAYER

Presider Lord God, it is through Christ we have been redeemed and in him we
were chosen. Continue to bless us and make us holy as we live as your
children. As your chosen ones may we always work to bring the reality
of your kingdom to those in our midst. We ask this through our Lord
Jesus Christ, your son, who lives and reigns with you and the Holy
Spirit, one God for ever and ever.
All Amen.

Your Attitude Must Be That of Christ

CALL TO WORSHIP

Presider   The grace of our Lord Jesus Christ ·and the love of God and the fellowship of the Holy Spirit be with you all.

All   And also with you.

THE WORD OF GOD

Reader   Philippians 2:1-11

INTERCESSIONS

Presider   Lord Jesus, you emptied yourself and took the form of a slave that we might have new life in you. Hear us now as we pray.
For the times we have acted out of rivalry and conceit.

All   Forgive us, Lord.

Presider   That our attitudes may always reflect the love you give
that we may be known as followers of Christ.

All   Forgive us, Lord.

Presider   May we be strong in our encounters with obstacles and temptations, strengthen our hearts and our minds.

All   Forgive us, Lord.

Presider   Let us never forget the poor and oppressed of our world,
guide us as we reach out to those in need.

All   Forgive us, Lord.

THE LORD'S PRAYER

Presider   Let us pray as Jesus did:
All   Our Father . . . .

CONCLUDING PRAYER

Presider   May the peace and glory of God which is beyond all understanding keep our hearts and minds in the knowledge and love of God and his Son, our Lord Jesus Christ.

All   Amen.

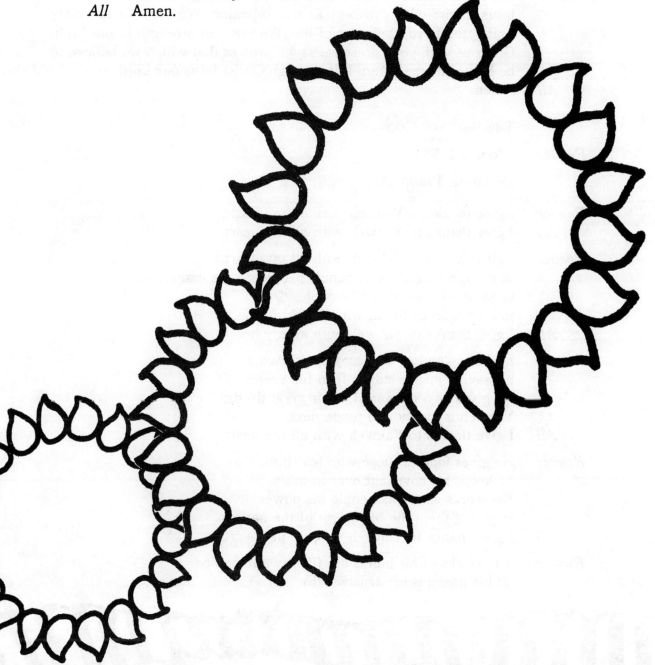

Those Who Believe Are Begotten of God

Presider   May God our loving creator grant you peace and faith.

All   Grace be with all who possess faith in our Lord Jesus Christ.

Presider   Let us pray. Lord God, we believe in your loving care and in our Lord Jesus Christ who you sent as our salvation. We trust in the Holy Spirit, the Lord, the giver of life. We pray for strength in our faith. Grace us with your presence as we profess that which we believe to be holy and true. Grant this through Christ Jesus our Lord.

All   Amen.

THE WORD OF GOD

Reader   1 John 5:1, 5-11

Response: Psalm 111

Reader   I give thanks to Yahweh with all my heart.

All   I give thanks to Yahweh with all my heart.

Reader   I give thanks to Yahweh with all my heart,
in the meeting-place of honest people, in the assembly.
Great are the deeds of Yahweh,
to be pondered by all who delight in them.

All   I give thanks to Yahweh with all my heart.

Reader   Full of splendour and majesty his work,
his saving justice stands firm for ever.
He gives us a memorial of his great deeds;
Yahweh is mercy and tenderness.

All   I give thanks to Yahweh with all my heart.

Reader   He gives food to those who fear him,
he keeps his covenant ever in mind.
His works show his people his power
in giving them the birthright of the nations.

All   I give thanks to Yahweh with all my heart.

Reader   The works of his hands are fidelity and justice,
all his precepts are trustworthy,

	established for ever and ever, accomplished in fidelity and honesty.
All	I give thanks to Yahweh with all my heart.
Reader	Deliverance he sends to his people, his covenant he imposes for ever; holy and awesome his name. The root of wisdom is fear of Yahweh; those who attain it are wise. His praise will continue for ever.
All	I give thanks to Yahweh with all my heart.

PROFESSION OF FAITH: Apostles' Creed

Presider	Let us profess that which we hold to be true:
All	I believe in God the Father Almighty, Creator of heaven and earth; and in Jesus Christ, His only Son, our Lord, Who was conceived by the Holy Spirit, born of the Virgin Mary, suffered under Pontius Pilate, was crucified, died, and was buried.
	He descended into hell; the third day He rose again from the dead.
	He ascended into heaven, sits at the right hand of God, the Father Almighty. From thence He shall come to judge the living and the dead.
	I believe in the Holy Spirit, the Holy Catholic church, the communion of saints, the forgiveness of sins, the resurrection of the body, and life everlasting. Amen.

INTERCESSIONS

Presider	In faith, let us pray to the Lord our God. (Spontaneous Prayers)

CONCLUDING PRAYER

Presider	Lord, we pray for all people who have faith in you. May we always be strong in faith, in hope and in love. May those who hesitate to believe be strengthened by our witness as we spread your love to all. We pray this in Jesus' name.
All	Amen.

Welcome the Word Within You

CALL TO WORSHIP

Presider   The Lord be with you.
All   And also with you.

Presider   Come, let us worship the Lord for he is our God and we are his people.
All   Be praised, Lord our God and Ruler of the universe, for bringing us to this day. Amen.

THE WORD OF GOD

Reader   James 1:16-27

INTERCESSIONS

Presider   Let us pray. Lord, hear the prayers of your people.
(Spontaneous Prayers)

THE LORD'S PRAYER

Presider   Let us together pray the prayer Jesus taught us.
All   Our Father . . . .

CONCLUDING PRAYER: Romans 16:25-27 (adapted)

Presider   Glory to him who is able to give us the strength to live according to the Good News, and in which we proclaim Jesus Christ, the revelation of a mystery kept secret for endless ages, but now so clear that it must be broadcast everywhere. This is only what scripture has predicted, and it is all part of the way the eternal God wants things to be. He alone is wisdom: give glory therefore to him through Jesus Christ for ever and ever.
All   Amen.

May The Gospel Continue To Grow In Your Midst

CALL TO WORSHIP

Presider   May the grace of our Lord Jesus Christ be with you all.
All   And also with you.

Presider   We gather in the presence of our God. May he hear our prayers and strengthen us.

THE WORD OF GOD

Reader   Colossians 1:3-14

Response: Psalm 100

Right   Acclaim Yahweh, all the earth,
serve Yahweh with gladness,
come into his presence with songs of joy!

Left   Be sure that Yahweh is God,
he made us, we belong to him,
his people, the flock of his sheepfold.

Right   Come within his gates giving thanks,
to his courts singing praise,
give thanks to him and bless his name!

Left   For Yahweh is good,
his faithful love is everlasting,
his constancy from age to age.

INTERCESSIONS

Presider   Let us pray. Lord, hear the prayers of your people.
(Spontaneous Prayers)

PRAYER OF PRAISE AND THANKSGIVING: Daniel 2:20-23

Presider   Having made known our needs, in praise and thanksgiving let us
bless our God as Daniel did:
All   Blessed be the name of God forever and ever,
for wisdom and power are his.
He causes the changes of the times and seasons,
makes kings and unmakes them.
He gives wisdom to the wise
and knowledge to those who understand.
He reveals deep and hidden things.
and knows what is in the darkness,
for the light dwells with him.
To you, O God, I give thanks and praise,
because you have given me wisdom and power.

CONCLUDING PRAYER

Presider   May he who is the Lord give us continued peace in every possible way.
All   Glory to the Father, and to the Son, and to the Holy Spirit:
As it was in the beginning, is now, and will be forever. Amen.

Through New Birth And Faith Salvation Will Be Yours

CALL TO WORSHIP

Presider   The grace and peace of God our Father and the Lord Jesus Christ be with you all.

All   Blessed be God, the Father of our Lord Jesus Christ.

THE WORD OF GOD

Reader   1 Peter 1:3-9

Response: Psalm 25

Reader   To you I lift up my soul, O Lord, my God.

All   To you I lift up my soul, O Lord, my God.

Reader   Adoration I offer, Yahweh,
to you, my God.
But in my trust in you do not put me to shame,
let not my enemies gloat over me.

All   To you I lift up my soul, O Lord, my God.

Reader   Calling to you, none shall ever be put to shame,
but shame is theirs who groundlessly break faith.
Direct me in your ways, Yahweh,
and teach me your paths.

All   To you I lift up my soul, O Lord, my God.

Reader   Encourage me to walk in your truth and teach me
since you are the God who saves me.
For my hope is in you all day long—
such is your generosity, Yahweh.
Goodness and faithful love have been yours for ever,

All   To you I lift up my soul, O Lord, my God.

Reader   Hold not my youthful sins against me,
but remember me as your faithful love dictates.

All   To you I lift up my soul, O Lord, my God.

PRAYERS OF PRAISE AND THANKSGIVING

Presider   Let us give praise and thanksgiving to God. (Spontaneous Prayers)

Response: We give thanks to you, O Lord.

THE LORD'S PRAYER

Presider Let us pray as Jesus did:
All Our Father . . . .

CONCLUDING PRAYER

Presider Almighty God, in your great mercy you give us new life through your Son, Jesus Christ. It is through this new birth and the faith we have been given that salvation will be ours. May our faith be strong and our mouths constantly give you praise, honor and glory forever.
All Amen. Alleluia!

Love Is of God

CALL TO WORSHIP

Presider The love of God and our Lord Jesus Christ be with you all.
All And also with you.

Presider Let us pray. Lord God, you so loved the world you sent your only Son that we might have life through him. He, in turn, has commanded us to live on in his love by loving one another. Dwell in us, Lord, and bring your love to perfection in us. Grant this through Christ our Lord.
All Amen.

THE WORD OF GOD

Reader 1 John 4:7-12

Response

Reader Great is the Lord and highly to be praised. All generations praise the works of the Lord.
All The love of the Lord is everlasting.

Reader The Lord is gracious and merciful, slow to anger and rich in kindness.

All   The love of the Lord is everlasting.

Reader   The Lord is good to all. The Lord shows compassion toward all his works.

All   The love of the Lord is everlasting.

INTERCESSIONS

Presider   Our God has loved us with an everlasting love and he answers those who call on him. In confidence, let us pray. (Spontaneous Prayers)

CONCLUDING PRAYER

Presider   God of infinite love, you revealed your love to us when you sent your only Son to be the sacrifice that takes away our sins. Yours is an everlasting love and you are constant in your affection toward us. May we respond to that love by reaching out to one another with compassion and understanding. We pray this in the name of our Lord Jesus Christ.

All   Amen.

Presider   May the peace and love of God be with us now and forever.

All   Amen.

Your Ways
Are Not My Ways

CALL TO WORSHIP

Presider   The Lord be with you.

All   And also with you.

Presider   Prepare our hearts and minds, O Lord, to accept your Word. Silence in us any voice that is not your own that in hearing we may also obey your will. We ask this in the name of the Lord Jesus Christ.

All   Amen.

THE WORD OF GOD

Reader   First Reading: Isaiah 55:6-9

Response: Psalm 15

Reader   He who does justice will live in the presence of the Lord.

All   He who does justice will live in the presence of the Lord.

Reader   Whoever lives blamelessly,
who acts uprightly.
who speaks the truth from the heart,
who keeps the tongue under control.

All   He who does justice will live in the presence of the Lord.

Reader   who does not wrong a comrade,
who casts no discredit on a neighbour,
who looks with scorn on the vile,
but honours those who fear Yahweh.

All   He who does justice will live in the presence of the Lord.

Reader   who stands by an oath at any cost,
who asks no interest on loans,
who takes no bribe to harm the innocent.
No one who so acts can ever be shaken.

All   He who does justice will live in the presence of the Lord.

Reader   Second Reading: Mark 7:1-8

INTERCESSIONS

Presider   Lord, we turn to you in need. Hear the prayers we offer to you. (Spontaneous Prayers)

THE LORD'S PRAYER

Presider   In confidence, let us pray as Jesus taught us:
All   Our Father . . . .

CONCLUDING PRAYER: Jude 24-25 (adapted)

Presider   There is but one God who can protect us from falling and bring us safely to his glorious presence. To God, the only God, who saves us through Christ Jesus our Lord, be glory, majesty, authority and power, now and for ages to come.
All   Amen.

Cleansed in the Waters
Of Baptism

CALL TO WORSHIP

Presider   The grace of the Lord Jesus Christ, the love of God and the fellowship of the Holy Spirit be with you.

All   And also with you.

Presider   Through our baptism we were welcomed into a community of believers. Cleansed in the waters of baptism, we shared in the death and resurrection of our Lord Jesus Christ and, in turn, were called to be disciples who continue the work of the Lord. United now in prayer, we recommit ourselves once again to the promises made on the day of baptism.

THE WORD OF GOD

Reader   Matthew 28:18-20

RENEWAL OF BAPTISMAL COMMITMENT

Presider   Let us renew the promises made in baptism when we rejected evil and promised to serve God faithfully.
Do you reject Satan?

All   I do.

Presider   And all his works?

All   I do.

Presider   And all his empty promises?

All   I do.

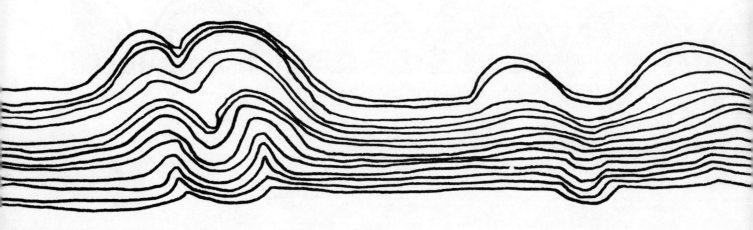

We further believe in God, the Father Almighty, creator of heaven and earth.

We believe in Jesus Christ, his only Son, our Lord, who was born of the Virgin Mary, was crucified, died, and was buried, rose from the dead, and is now seated at the right hand of the Father.

We believe in the Holy Spirit, the holy Catholic Church, the communion of saints, the forgiveness of sins, the resurrection of the body, and life everlasting.

Presider   The God of our Lord Jesus Christ has given us new life by water and the Holy Spirit and has forgiven our sins. May we be faithful to our Lord Jesus Christ now and for ever.

All   Amen.

INTERCESSIONS

Presider   Let us pray to the Lord our God. (Spontaneous Prayers)

CONCLUDING PRAYER

Presider   Through water and the Holy Spirit, we are reborn to everlasting life. In God's goodness, may he continue to bless us. May he make us always faithful members of his holy people. May he grace us with peace now and always in Christ Jesus our Lord.

All   Amen.

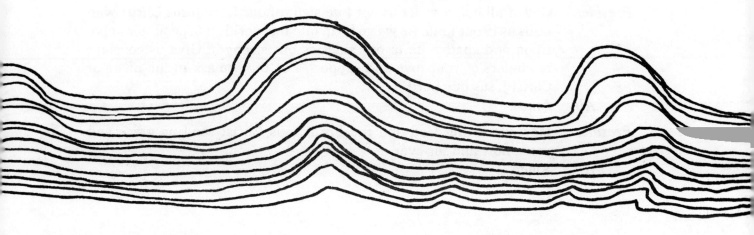

Do Not Lose Sight
Of Christ Jesus

CALL TO WORSHIP

Presider Sing praise to the Lord in the assembly of the faithful.

All He sends us forth to live in hope and peace until we gather again.

THE WORD OF GOD

Reader Hebrews 12:1-3

Response: Daniel 3:52, 82-87, 89-90 (adapted)

Reader Blessed are you O Lord, the God of our fathers and mothers.
Be praised and exalted above all forever.
Blessed is your holy and glorious name.

Children of the Lord, bless the Lord.

All Glory and praise to you, O Lord.

Reader Servants of the Lord, bless the Lord.

All Glory and praise to you, O Lord.

Reader Spirits and souls of the just, bless the Lord.

All Glory and praise to you, O Lord.

Reader Holy people of humble heart, bless the Lord.

All Glory and praise to you, O Lord.

Reader Give thanks to the Lord, for he is good and his mercy endures
forever. All who worship him, bless the God of gods, for his love is
everlasting.

CONCLUDING PRAYER

Presider God of all holiness, let us not lose sight of our Lord Jesus Christ who
leads us in our faith. As we go forth into the world and encounter oppo-
sition and apathy, be at our sides as our strength. Give us constant
reminders of your love and support. For this we ask in the name of
Christ Jesus our Lord.

All Amen.

Presider May our loving God and the Lord Jesus Christ send us grace and
peace now and for ever.

All Amen.

Receive a Blessing As Your Inheritance

CALL TO WORSHIP

Presider Let us rejoice in the Lord.
All And bless his holy name.

Presider Let us pray. Lord, as we go forth from this gathering we ask that you bless us and make us holy. Called to seek peace and love one another, we pray that wisdom and kindness guide our actions as we depart. Be with us now and always and grant us your grace and mercy in the name of Jesus the Lord.
All Amen.

THE WORD OF GOD

Reader 1 Peter 3:8-12

INTERCESSIONS

Presider Let us pray. (Spontaneous Prayers)

THE LORD'S PRAYER

Presider Gathering our prayers into one, let us pray:
All Our Father in heaven,
may your name be held holy,
your kingdom come,
your will be done
on earth as in heaven.
Give us today our daily bread.
And forgive us our debts,
as we have forgiven those who are in debt to us.
And do not put us to the test,
but save us from the evil one.

CONCLUDING PRAYER

Presider May the peace of our Lord be with you always.
All And also with you.
Presider As we go forth may the Lord bless us, protect us from all evil and bring us to everlasting life.
All Amen.